CHARTRES

THE CATHEDRAL AND THE OLD TOWN

TEXT BY MALCOLM MILLER, Lecturer and Guide to the Cathedral
PHOTOGRAPHS BY SONIA HALLIDAY & LAURA LUSHINGTON

CHARTRES

THE CATHEDRAL AND THE OLD TOWN

From afar, the cathedral of Our Lady of Chartres appears as a mysterious vessel, floating in the distant haze upon fields of waving wheat. It is not until the last moment, of a sudden, over the brow of a last hill, that the city is discovered, spread at her feet like a patchwork quilt of pepper-tiled roof tops, pinnacles, gables and steeples. Half-timbered and limestone houses crowd narrow winding streets that slope steeply towards the river, which is straddled by a series of hump-backed bridges. It is over such bridges and up such winding streets that chanting pilgrims have come for a thousand years to pay homage to the Queen of Heaven in her terrestrial palace; it is here that St Bernard came to preach a crusade, and the French king Henry IV to be crowned; it is here, in a bygone age, to this city renowned for its learning, that students came to hear the masters of Chartres teach; and where, still today, pilgrim and scholar mingle with all the others who come to hear Chartres speak of truth and beauty, time and eternity – the city of man and the city of God.

The history of Chartres and its cathedral

Although there is archaeological evidence that Autricum (Roman Chartres), built upon the Autura (Eure) river, was comparatively important, with an amphitheatre and two aqueducts, nothing is known of its religious life, or its evangelization by the first Christians. Bishops of Chartres attended the early 6th-century synods at Orleans, but the first reference to a cathedral is not until 743, when Hunald, Duke of Aquitaine, having quarrelled with Charles Martel's sons, sacked the city, and its cathedral was destroyed. The second known cathedral, already dedicated to Mary, was burnt by Hastings, a Viking, when he pillaged the city in 858, and the third, quickly rebuilt with a raised choir over a martyrium, was probably consecrated in 876, when Charlemagne's grandson, Charles the Bald, presented Chartres with its famous holy relic, the Sancta Camisia, now in the cathedral treasury.

This piece of cloth, which Mary was supposed to have worn when she gave birth to Christ, was soon to make Chartres into one of the most popular pilgrimage shrines of medieval Europe, and its citizens knew not only that the relic was a considerable source of income for them, but also that they, and their city, were protected through it by Mary. Thus, in 911, when Chartres was besieged by Rollon, another Viking warrior, Bishop Gantelme displayed the relic upon the city ramparts. Rollon then

*

LEFT: *A king and queen of Judah. Royal Portal, mid-12th century.*

FACING PAGE: *A peaceful river scene.*

fled, made his peace with King Charles III, was converted to Christianity and invested as first Duke of Normandy. His descendant, Richard, Duke of Normandy, profiting from the absence of Thibault the Cheat, the most famous of the counts of Chartres, with whom he was at war, pillaged and burnt most of the city in 962.

At that time the defences extended along the crest of the hill high above the Eure river, from the cathedral and the counts' castle (demolished between 1802 and 1817), to where the apse of St Aignan's Church stands today, but the monastery of St-Père-en-Vallée, famous for its teaching, was outside the city walls. The Benedictine monks left during the French Revolution, but their church still stands, although its name was changed from St Père to St Pierre (St Peter).

The intellectual reputation of Chartres was considerably enhanced by the arrival, in 990, of Fulbert – 'the venerable Socrates of the Chartres Academy' – to teach at the cathedral school, which for the next 200 years was to be one of the great scholastic institutions of medieval Europe, until the founding of the University of Paris in 1215 caused it to decline. Amongst Fulbert's intellectual suc-

cessors were Bernard of Chartres, chancellor from 1119 to 1124, followed by Gilbert de la Porrée until 1141, then by Bernard's younger brother, Thierry of Chartres. St Ivo of Chartres (1040–1117) and the Englishman John of Salisbury (1110–80), the secretary of Thomas à Becket, like Fulbert died as illustrious bishops of Chartres.

It was during the bishopric of Fulbert that a great fire destroyed the cathedral, in September 1020. By 1024 an enormous new crypt had been completed, which is still the largest in France. With funds provided by King Robert of France, Canute of England and Denmark, William IV, Duke of Aquitaine, Richard, Duke of Normandy, and Eudes, Count of Chartres-Blois, the new Romanesque cathedral, with nave, aisles, apsidal chapels, a north tower, west porch and bell-tower, was almost completed at the time of Fulbert's death in 1028, but, because of another fire in 1030, the dedication ceremony was delayed until 1037.

A century later, during the episcopates of Geoffrey de Lèves (1115–49) and Goslein de Musy (1149–56), Fulbert's cathedral was extended westwards, firstly by constructing a single free-standing north-west tower, orig-

inally with a steeple in wood (but today supporting the flamboyant structure (1506–13) built by Jean Texier). Then, during the ensuing decades, a south-west tower was built with an elegantly proportioned octagonal stone steeple, which soared up over a much lower church than the present one. The crypts were lengthened into the two new towers, and between them a magnificent portal sculpted

*

LEFT: *The Jesse window, about 1150. From the groin of Jesse, who reclines at the foot of the window, springs a stem in the branches of which sit four kings of Judah, then Mary, and Christ at the top, surrounded by seven doves symbolizing the Seven Gifts of the Holy Spirit. In the border are twice seven Old Testament prophets, who foretold that Christ would come from the House of David.*

TOP: *St Peter and St James. Detail from a 12th-century mural in Fulbert's Romanesque crypt.*

ABOVE: *The Sancta Camisia, given to Chartres in 876 by King Charles the Bald and thought to have been worn by Mary when she gave birth to Christ. The reliquary is modern.*

(1145–55), known as the Royal Portal, surmounted by three lancet windows, amongst the finest to have survived from medieval Europe.

The Gothic cathedral

During the night of 10 June 1194 yet another fire destroyed the city of Chartres, and Fulbert's cathedral was very severely damaged. Only the crypts, the newly completed western towers and Royal Portal survived. The tragedy is narrated in detail in the *Book of the Miracles of the Virgin*, written in the mid-13th century and translated somewhat later by Jehan Lemarchand into medieval French.

At first, we are told, the people despaired, because they believed that Mary's precious relic had also burned, and therefore that her protection of the city was lost; but, on the third day after the fire, Cardinal Melior of Pisa, a papal legate who was in Chartres on the night of the fire, assembled everyone in front of the smouldering cathedral and was exhorting them to build a new shrine for Mary, when a procession appeared with the relic safe. The cardinal then proclaimed that this was a sign from Mary that she desired a more magnificent church, and great enthusiasm was immediately aroused for the reconstruction.

People gathered voluntarily in the

quarries at Berchères-les-Pierres and dragged carts laden with stone a distance of five miles to the building site. Bishop Regnaud de Mouçon and the cathedral chapter gave up the most part of their considerable income over the next five years for the building of the new cathedral. King Philip Augustus, who visited Chartres in 1210, provided each year the funds needed for the construction of the North Porch, continued by his son, Louis VIII, whose queen, Blanche of Castille, regent of France from 1226 to 1236, donated the North Rose window and lancets. Their son, Saint Louis, gave a rood screen, unfortunately demolished by the 18th-century clergy. (Fragments, however, can be seen in the cathedral treasury.)

Richard Coeur de Lion, although at war with Philip Augustus, permitted priests to fund-raise in England. Other gifts came from a king of Castille, probably Ferdinand III, who is portrayed in one of the choir rose windows, as are Prince Louis of France, son of Philip Augustus, and other mounted knights in armour, all facing east as though setting out upon a crusade to the Holy Land and bearing the coats-of-arms of their noble families, Beaumont, Courtenay and Montfort. Pierre Mauclerc, Count of Dreux and Duke of Brittany, gave the South Rose, and can be seen with his

family kneeling beside their heraldry at the base of the five lancets beneath the rose, which they also gave. More of the choir glass was offered by the Count of Chartres, Thibault VI.

The city of Chartres in the 12th and 13th centuries
The merchant donors

Although Chartres was not recognized as a commune until the end of the 13th century, it was a very prosperous city, administered jointly by the count and the bishop, which was the cause of occasional friction. As the feudal system declined, there had been a drifting away from the land towards the developing towns, which became increasingly important trading centres. Chartres was no exception, and new city ramparts had been constructed just before the 1194 fire to contain the growing population, especially along the river. Great fairs were held on the four feast days of the Virgin, her Nativity, Annunciation, Purification and Assumption, and certain merchants enjoyed the privileges and protection of the cathedral close, which, a city within the city, was outside the jurisdiction of the count. Thus an amicable relationship existed between the cathedral chapter and the city traders.

The merchant brotherhoods, in fact, donated 42 windows for the new cathedral, and their 'signatures', more than 100 scenes showing their occupations, provide a fascinating insight into everyday life in the early 13th century. So generous and continuous were these gifts pouring in, that the debris of the ruined cathedral was soon cleared, and master-builders and craftsmen were able to set up their workshops and begin reconstructing. So quickly did they build that by 1220 William the Breton, the court chronicler, wrote of the new cathedral in his *Philippis*:

'None can be found in the whole world that would equal its structure, its size and decor . . . the Mother of Christ has a special love for this one church, granting a minor place, as it were, to all other churches . . . None is shining so brightly than this nowadays, rising anew and complete with dressed stone, already finished up to the level of the vault, it will never fear any damage by fire till the day of the Judgment arrives.'

Romanesque crypt and Gothic architecture

Fulbert's 11th-century crypt was strengthened, especially in the apse, by doubling the wall around the three

Continued on page 12

ABOVE: *Detail from the window of the Incarnation, about 1150. In the lower row, from left to right, are scenes of the Annunciation, the Visitation and the Nativity, where the Child is placed not in a manger but on an altar to symbolize His future sacrifice. Above, on the left, the angels appear to the shepherds in the fields with their dogs. In the centre and right-hand scenes, the Magi stand before Herod asking 'Where is he that is born King of the Jews?', while beneath the arch on the left a scribe and a Pharisee consult the Scriptures.*

*

RIGHT: *Two of the monthly labours – July reaping and April holding the branches of a tree covered with leaves and blossom. Above them are the corresponding zodiac signs, Cancer and Aries. From the left bay of the Royal Portal.*

*

FACING PAGE: *Detail from the Passion and Resurrection window, about 1150. At the bottom left is the Betrayal, where the kiss of Judas, the seizure of Christ and the cutting off of Malchus's ear are combined in a violent composition. On the right Jesus, tied to a column and wearing the crown of thorns, is viciously scourged by two men brandishing huge whips. Above, on the left, Mary and John the Apostle contemplate Jesus on the cross, the wood of which, by virtue of His life-giving sacrifice, has become a living green. On the right, Christ is taken down from the cross by Joseph of Arimathea while Nicodemus removes the nails from His feet.*

7

ABOVE: *The Cellier de Loëns is one of the finest examples in France of late 12th-century architecture. It was used until the 18th century as a tithe barn, where the clergy stored their wine. A long flight of steps leads down into a magnificently vaulted room, with a series of circular columns that support ogival arches and crossed ribs. Above is another large room remarkable for its 14th-century timberwork. The Grenier de Loëns now houses the exhibitions of the International Stained Glass Centre.*

*

LEFT: *The Tertre Saint-Nicolas, a picturesque flight of steps leading from the cathedral down to St Andrew's Church.*

*

FACING PAGE: *The present church of St Andrew, here reflected in the River Eure, dates mostly from the 12th century. An earlier structure, probably founded in 960, burnt in 1134, leaving two crypts beneath the transept. During the 13th century St Andrew's was extended by building a bridge spanning the river, upon which Jehan de Beauce built a choir in the 16th century. In 1612 an apsidal chapel was added by building another bridge over the rue du Massacre (named after the slaughterhouse which used to stand there). This chapel collapsed in 1805 and for safety reasons the choir was demolished in 1827. The church was used as a depot by the Germans in the Second World War and much damaged by fire.*

ABOVE: *The cathedral seen from the south-east, towering over the colourful rooftops of Chartres.*

FACING PAGE: *The interior of the cathedral by floodlight. The nave is unusually wide, owing to the dimensions of the Romanesque crypt upon which the Gothic cathedral was built, and its ceiling vaults reach a height of 37 metres.*

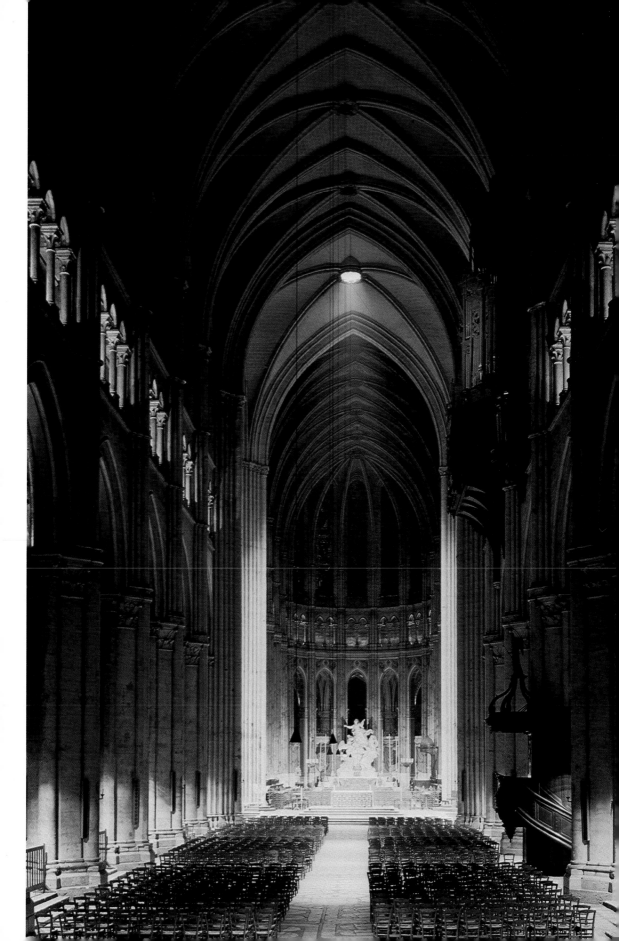

wide, barrel-vaulted chapels, and adding late 12th-century rib-vaulted ones between them. These alternating Romanesque and Gothic, wide and narrow chapels in the crypt predetermined the semicircular apsidal form of the Gothic cathedral above and the disposition of its radiating chapels, just as the long, groin-vaulted galleries beneath the aisles of the Gothic church predetermined its width and orientation, and the decision to keep the mid-12th-century Royal Portal and its flanking towers predetermined its length. The Gothic architects, however, did expand in two ways; firstly by adding a very wide transept, so that the ground plan symbolically forms a Latin cross, and secondly by building much higher.

The interior elevation is tripartite, with arcade, triforium and clerestory. The lower storey, or arcade, is made up of a series of pointed arches, or ogives, in the nave, transept and choir. They support the triforium, a horizontal narrow gallery, with a row of elegant columns giving a vertical rhythm, replacing the heavy tribunes of earlier cathedrals that extended back over the whole width of the aisle. Above the triforium, the clerestory, or top storey, is lit by a series of double lancet windows with a small cusped rose window above. Alternating circular piers with octagonal shafts and octagonal piers with circular shafts divide the nave, transept and choir into rectangular bays. The front shafts cut through the capitals, decorated with crockets and foliage, thereby emphasizing verticality, and support transverse arches that span the structure from wall to wall.

Crossed ribs, with central sculpted circular hollow key-stones, which still show traces of paint and gilt, divide the roof into quadripartite rectangular vaults. Where the ribs and transverse arches abut the shoulder of the building, flying buttresses outside stabilize their thrust. This system made it both possible to build higher and to open up the walls to a degree not before dared, and fill them with stained glass, so that they appear, like the walls of the Heavenly Jerusalem, to be 'garnished with all manner of precious stones' (Rev. 21:19, 20).

The stained glass

With the three west lancets, c.1150, the famous Notre-Dame de la Belle Verrière, or Blue Virgin, c.1180, and more than 150 early 13th-century windows, Chartres possesses by far the most complete collection of medieval stained glass, forming an incomparable documentation of life and faith in the Middle Ages.

Set like giant transparent illuminated manuscripts in walls of Berchères limestone, the Chartres windows are peopled with kings and princes and great ladies of the court in fine raiments of silk and ermine and cloth of gold. There are knights in coat of mail, and priests in richly embroidered vestments of ruby, saffron, azure and emerald. Peasants in smocks of coarse cloth, hooded against the March winds, or stripped to the waist for the August harvest, are caught timelessly in their seasonal occupations, just as various artisans, tool in hand, sculpt stone, weave or fashion wood in their workshops, for ever. Fishmongers beneath a colourful umbrella, butchers and bakers offer their goods for sale. Furriers and drapers proudly display their wares. A farrier shoes a horse, set in a wooden frame, a cobbler laces boots, and a vintner prunes his vine.

Tales are told of heroic deeds: how Charlemagne defeated the Moors and Roland slew the infidel Ferragut; and saintly lives from the Golden Legend exemplify the virtues needed in this world in order to triumph upon the human condition, and at the Final Judgment enter the next, the eternal Heavenly Jerusalem. St Nicholas and St Martin, for example, illustrate charity; St Eustace and other martyrs remain constant to their faith, in spite of terrible adversity. Mary Magdalene and St Julian are repentant sinners, who receive their reward in the Kingdom of Heaven.

The moral implications of such windows would be understood by all,

Continued on page 18

★

FACING PAGE AND RIGHT: *Three details from early 13th-century stained-glass windows showing donors from the merchant brotherhoods at their occupations: butchers, who gave the Miracles of Mary window; a wheelwright, donor of the Noah window; and sculptors, donors of the St Chéron window.*

ABOVE: *Detail from the Charlemagne window. In the lower circle, Charlemagne orders the building of a church to St James in Pamplona. Above, on the right, is the miraculous blossoming of the lances of those soldiers who are to die at the battle of Roncevaux and, on the left, the battle itself. In the diamond is the joust between Roland and Ferragut. Above, on the left, Roland slays Ferragut and, on the right, Charlemagne returns to France. In the upper circle, Roland blows his horn and then, mortally wounded, he tries to destroy his sword, Durandal, against a rock.*

13

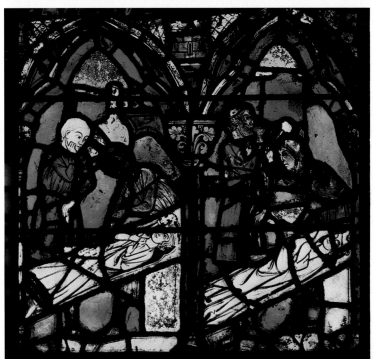

ABOVE LEFT: *St Piat, a local martyr, and St George, whose death upon the wheel is depicted on the pedestal. Left bay of the South Porch.*

★

ABOVE RIGHT: *The martyrdom of St Thomas Becket. Left bay of the South Porch.*

★

LEFT: *Pride falling from his horse. From the left bay of the South Porch, right pier, south face.*

★

FACING PAGE: *Figures from the right jamb of the central bay of the South Porch, early 13th century. From left to right, the apostles Paul, John, James the Greater, James the Less, Bartholomew and Matthew. Beyond, in the right bay, can be seen the confessors St Gregory and St Avitus.*

14

ABOVE: *The churches of St Peter and St Aignan, from across the river.*

FACING PAGE: *The apse and altar of St Peter's Church. The Benedictine monastery of Saint-Père-en-Vallée was disestablished during the French Revolution and its church renamed St Pierre (St Peter). The monastery is first mentioned in the 7th century as having received a* donation *from St Bathilde, the wife of Clovis II. It was rebuilt in the 10th century by Benedictine monks from Fleury (now Saint-Benoît-sur-Loire) and the bell-tower probably dates from that time. After the fire of 1134, Abbot Hilduard built the lower parts of the present choir, the ambulatory and apsidal chapels. The north side of the nave was constructed next, at the end of the 12th century; the* south side during the early 13th century; and Hilduard's choir vaulted in the mid-13th century, with an unusual clerestory-triforium, today lit by 16th-century glass from the neighbouring church of St Hilaire, demolished during the French Revolution. The 29 late 13th- and early 14th-century windows of St Peter's Church constitute one of Europe's finest collections of medieval stained glass.*

whereas the much more complex symbolic or typological interpretations of some of the biblical windows would probably only be fully comprehended by the scholars, through their acquaintance with the exegetic writings of the Church fathers and doctors, such as St Augustine, St Jerome and St Ambrose of Milan, or of early medieval commentators such as the Venerable Bede and Isidore of Seville. Hence, Noah as saviour, Joseph betrayed and forgiving, David, a new king of the Jews, Moses as lawgiver or Solomon in his wisdom are examples of Christ prefigurations. Similarly, parables, such as that of the Good Samaritan, were interpreted symbolically. Thus, according to the Venerable Bede, the man left wounded on the wayside represents humanity, spiritually wounded because of the fault of Adam and Eve, the Samaritan is Christ the Redeemer, the inn symbolizes the Church, and the promise to return and settle debts, Judgment Day.

The 12th and 13th-century sculpture

Solemnly, the screen of rigid column figures of the west Royal Portal (1145–

55), like the actors of a mystery play upon the cathedral steps, appear about to speak their parts; with raised hand, to proclaim a great prophecy, or, as a queen of Judah, just to smile, serenely, in the knowledge that her lineage will bring forth the Christ. Then, over their heads, come more than 200 figurines to narrate the great mysteries of Christ's birth and death, his ascension and return in glory at the end of time, with brief intervals to portray the menial and the intellectual labours of this world.

Like petrified players from the early 13th century, the statues of the north and south porches enact the Divine Comedy, from the beginning of the world to its end, from the Creation and Fall to the Final Judgment, from Paradise Lost to Paradise Regained. (See Malcolm Miller, *Chartres Cathedral, The Medieval Stained Glass and Sculpture*, Pitkin Pictorials, 1980.)

If the stained glass reminded medieval man of the precious stones, as described by St John, that garnish the walls of the City of God, then the sculpted portals and porches outside, richly gilded and painted, the en-

trances to this city, built on earth, represent the Gates of Heaven. This is no exaggeration, for it is known that in medieval times, on dedication day, a new church was likened to the Heavenly Jerusalem, and the appropriate passages were read out to the people from the Book of the Revelation.

The project of building nine steeples was abandoned, and on 17 or 24 October 1260, undoubtedly amongst great rejoicing and pageantry, the new cathedral was dedicated to the Assumption of Our Lady, a worthy palace for the Queen of Heaven.

Chartres and its cathedral since 1260

The admirable unity of Chartres Cathedral, both architectural and iconographical, is primarily due to the speed with which it was constructed, and then to its having survived, almost unscathed, 16th-century fanaticism, the 18th-century French Revolution and the 20th-century world wars, with only minor additions or alterations during 700 years.

The 14th century

After the addition of a vestry in the mid-13th century, east of the north transept, the first 14th-century extension to the cathedral was the St Piat Chapel, built between 1324 and 1353, where pilgrims flocked to the saint's miraculous relic by climbing an elegant staircase opened up between the east and south-east apsidal chapels. (Today the St Piat Chapel exhibits the cathedral treasure, which includes Mary's relic and fragments of the 13th-century rood screen.)

Meanwhile, in 1286, the county of Chartres had been sold by the Countess Jeanne to King Philip the Fair, who then, in 1293, offered it to his brother, Charles de Valois, already Count of Alençon and Anjou. His

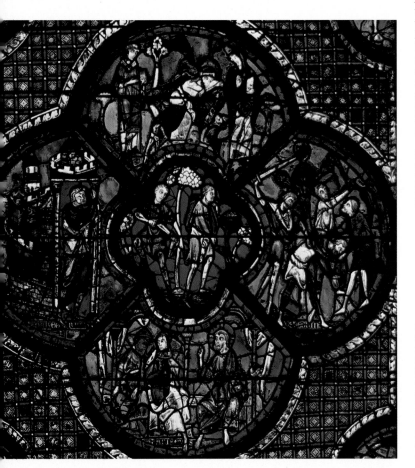

LEFT: *Detail from the Good Samaritan window. In the lower semicircle Jesus is narrating the parable. On the left, a man leaves Jerusalem and takes the road to Jericho, but thieves (in the centre and on the right) attack him, strip him of his goods and leave him wounded. In the upper semicircle, a priest and a Levite walk by without helping.*

FACING PAGE: *Flying buttresses on the south side of the choir make a complex and delicate pattern.*

ABOVE: *Four of the monthly labours from the right bay of the North Porch:* (top row, from left to right) *February warming his feet by a fire; March pruning a vine; May with a hawk upon his wrist;* (bottom row, left) *June with a scythe.* Bottom row, centre and right: *stripping flax and carding – scenes of 'active life' from the left bay of the North Porch.*

FACING PAGE: *The left jamb of the central bay of the North Porch, early 13th century, with figures from the Old Testament who prefigure Christ's sacrifice on the cross. From left to right: Melchizedek, like Christ both priest and king, holding a chalice with bread and wine; Abraham preparing to sacrifice his son Isaac, as* Christ *was later sacrificed by His father; Moses, the lawgiver, pointing to the brazen serpent, a symbol for Christ's death on the cross; Aaron or Samuel killing a lamb, another symbol of Christ's sacrifice; and David, prophet of Christ's Passion, carrying the lance and crown of thorns. On the right are St Peter and Elijah.*

descendant Philip de Valois was crowned Philip VI of France at Rheims on 29 May 1328, and Chartres for the next 200 years was directly attached to the crown. Louis XIII raised Chartres to a duchy, and it then remained in the Orleans family until the French Revolution.

The choice of Philip de Valois as king of France, and not Edward III of England, a grandson of Philip the Fair of France, brought about the Hundred Years War. Froissart in his *Chronicles* tells how in 1360 Edward's army was encamped near Chartres when a terrible hail storm killed men and horses alike. Edward then came to Chartres, made a generous offering to the cathedral and vowed to Our Lady that he would make peace, and the Treaty of Brétigny was signed!

It was largely because of the Hundred Years War that the city walls had to be strengthened and in 1356 a moat dug out as an extra defence. Nine gates then existed. With the exception of William's Gate (Porte Guillaume) which survived until 1944, when it was blown up by the retreating Nazis, the others, with most of the ramparts and the counts' castle, were demolished in the early 19th century, leaving only their names, such as Porte Cendreuse (Ash Wednesday Gate), Porte Drouaise (Dreux Gate) or Porte Châtelet.

Similarly, many of the street names, especially to the south of the cathedral, still indicate the trades that took place in them: for example, rue des Changes (money changers), rue aux Herbes (herbs), rue de la Petite Cordonnerie (shoemakers), place de la Poissonnerie (fish market), rue de la Tonnellerie (coopers).

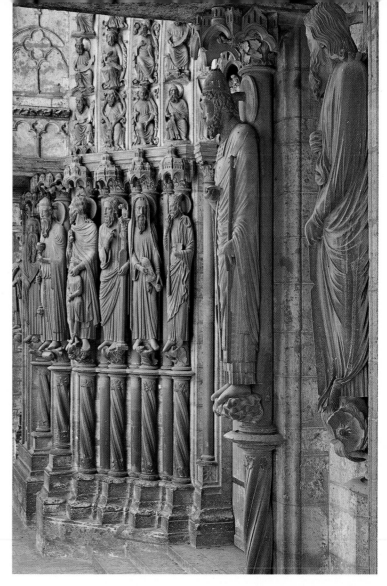

Between the collegiate church of St Andrew and the Benedictine monastery of St-Père-en-Vallée, a series of mills was constructed along the river, where the wool and leather trades prospered, a fact which, again, is reflected in such street names as rue de la Tannerie (tanners), rue de la Corroierie (straps and belts) and rue de la Foulerie (fullers). The grain market (place des Halles), even until the 20th century, was one of the most important in France.

The 15th century

In 1413, Louis de Bourbon, Count of Vendôme, having been imprisoned by his brother Jacques and threatened with death and the confiscation of his estates, once released made a vow to Our Lady to raise a chapel in her honour in Chartres Cathedral. Construction of the Vendôme Chapel was begun the same year, and continued even though Louis had been captured

again, this time by Henry V Plantagenet of England, at the Battle of Agincourt.

In 1417 Chartres fell to the Anglo-Burgundians and was then occupied until 12 April 1432, when liberated by Dunois and others, serving Joan of Arc. Henry Plantagenet, meanwhile, having been recognized as successor to the French throne in 1421, walked bare-footed, candle in hand, from Dreux to Chartres on Assumption Day of that year.

Other royal pilgrims and benefactors were Charles VII and Louis XI, who came to Chartres many times between 1462 and 1481, as did Anne de Bretagne, queen of both Charles VIII and his successor, Louis XII of the House of Orleans.

The 16th century

It was largely due to the munificence of Louis XII, who gave 2,000 livres,

and the publishing of indulgences by the Papal legate, Cardinal Georges d'Amboise, to all those who helped, whether by their labours or offerings, that work was begun in 1507 upon the construction of a new steeple for the north tower, the old wooden one covered in lead having been struck by lightning, and burnt.

Jean Texier, known as Jehan de Beauce, was appointed architect, and, having completed the new spire by 1513 in the richly ornate flamboyant Gothic style of his day, he was then commissioned to build a choir screen in the same style, which he began in 1514 and worked upon until his death on 29 December 1529. The sculpted groups within this screen, however, took two centuries to complete, depending upon the availability of funds.

Work upon this screen might easily have been abandoned in 1568, and the medieval glass and sculpture

Continued on page 26

21

ABOVE: *The North Rose window, about 1230, given by Queen Blanche of Castille, whose coats of arms decorate the spandrels. The figures in the five lancet windows are Melchizedek and Nebuchadnezzar, David and Saul, St Anne, Solomon and Jeroboam, then Aaron and* *his persecutor the Pharaoh, who is falling into the Red Sea. The rose window is composed of 12 semicircles containing the 12 minor prophets and 12 squares with 12 kings of Judah; doves and angels surround the central figure of the Virgin and Child.* FACING PAGE: *The west front of the cathedral, showing the 12th-century Royal Portal, towers and south steeple; the 13th-century West Rose and gallery of French kings above it; and the early 16th-century north steeple in flamboyant Gothic. (Photograph by Martine Klotz)*

ABOVE: *The St Piat Chapel, added in the early 14th century, now houses the cathedral treasure, which includes Mary's* *relic and fragments of the 13th-century rood-screen given by Saint Louis and demolished in the 18th century.* FACING PAGE: *An attractive view down the river to St Andrew's Church, with ancient wash-houses.*

destroyed and the holy relics thrown to the wind in the name of religious fanaticism, had not the city withstood the siege of the Prince de Condé and his Huguenot army, in spite of a breach in the city walls near the Dreux Gate. This district has ever since been known as 'La Brèche' (the Breach).

In 1588, Henry III sought refuge in Chartres, having fled Paris after the Day of the Barricades (12 May). He had been a frequent pilgrim to Our Lady of Chartres between 1579 and 1588, and rented two houses in front of the Royal Portal. He had been preceded by other royal pilgrims, the young Queen of Scotland, Mary Stuart, betrothed to Francis II of France, and by his own father, Henry II, in 1555, accompanied by the Duke and Duchess of Guise.

It was the Guise family which founded the League in 1576 to defend Catholicism against the Calvinists, but also to overthrow Henry III and place themselves upon the French throne. Before his assassination in 1589, Henry III acknowledged Henry of Navarre as his successor, but the new king had to struggle for his throne. In 1591 he besieged Chartres, which

favoured the League, but the city resisted for two months before capitulating. Several cannon balls hit the cathedral, one smashing a statue of the Gallery of Kings, and another passing through the West Rose to land in the choir. For a while it was decided to sing Mass in the crypts!

In 1593, Henry abjured Calvinism and, Rheims remaining in the hands of the League, he was crowned Henry IV of France in Chartres Cathedral, on 27 February 1594.

The 18th century

Having survived the 16th-century wars of religion almost unharmed and passed through a comparatively uneventful 17th century, except for the visits of Louis XIII, Anne d'Autriche and Louis XIV, Chartres Cathedral then, in the latter half of the 18th century, suffered the greatest degradations and indignities of its history, firstly at the hands of the clergy, then at those of the revolutionaries.

In 1753, the cathedral chapter decided to 'modernize' the choir. The borders of several of the 13th-century choir windows were removed and plain glass inserted. In 1763 the rood screen, offered by Saint Louis, was de-

molished, and wrought-iron gates took its place. Bridan, in 1773, sculpted the Assumption high altar, and eight of the choir windows and four in the transept were destroyed to let in more light. (Today the eight choir windows have early 20th-century grisaille glass, and two of the transept windows now contain stained glass made by the Chartres artist François Lorin, one offered by the American Architects' Association in 1954 and the other by the German Friends of Chartres Society in 1971.)

During the French Revolution and the ensuing Terror the very rich cathedral treasure was despoiled, a constitutional clergy established, the Episcopal Palace transformed into local government offices, the much revered Romanesque wooden statue of Our Lady of the Crypt burnt in front of the Royal Portal on 20 December 1793, and the cathedral rededicated as a 'Temple of Reason'.

Continued on page 32

*

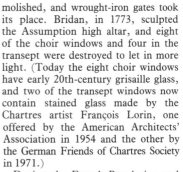

LEFT: *An early 16th-century house in the rue des Ecuyers with a remarkable external carved spiral structure known as Queen Berthe's staircase. Countess of Chartres by her first marriage, Berthe then married King Robert II (996-1031). Although the castle of the counts of Chartres stood above the ramparts just behind it, there can obviously be no link in fact between Queen Berthe and this Renaissance house.*

FACING PAGE, ABOVE: *The Siege of Chartres by the Prince de Condé and his Huguenot army in 1568. (Reproduced by courtesy of the Curator of the Chartres museum)*

FACING PAGE, BELOW: *The Episcopal Palace, now the Chartres museum. The first known palace here was built by Bishop Ivo in 1100 and destroyed like the cathedral in the 1194 fire. A new palace was built, where most of the kings of France stayed when on pilgrimage to Chartres, as did Henry IV before his coronation on 27 February 1594. Although some parts are earlier, most of the present building dates from the 17th and 18th centuries. Behind the palace, pleasant gardens spread down towards the river.*

The interior, with its fine two-branch staircase with wrought-iron ramps, its Italian room surrounded by a balcony, its reception rooms and chapel, is especially elegant.

The museum houses impressive collections of French and Flemish tapestries, enamels including the Apostles by Léonard Limosin I, paintings by artists such as Holbein, Zurbarán and Van Loo, coins and armour. There are also sections on local history and archaeology.

FACING PAGE: *The south ambulatory of the cathedral, showing part of the choir screen constructed by Jehan de Beauce between 1514 and 1529. The 41 sculpted* *scenes took two centuries to complete and are the work of various artists. The screen begins and ends with scenes from the life of Mary; in between are scenes from the* *life of Christ.*

ABOVE: *Mary sewing. An enchanting sculpture by Jean Soulas from the choir screen, about 1520.*

ABOVE: *The 19th-century altar of Our Lady of the Pillar. The painted pear-wood statue of the Virgin, traditionally clothed, probably dates from the 16th century.*

*

LEFT: *The high altar, sculpted by Charles-Antoine Bridan in 1767-73, represents the Assumption of Mary, to which Chartres Cathedral is dedicated, and is clearly influenced by Italian sculpture, in particular the work of Bernini.*

*

FACING PAGE: *The author's 15th-century home in the rue des Ecuyers was one of the first of the many half-timbered and gabled houses of old Chartres to be restored in the 1970s. The rue des Ecuyers ran beneath the counts' castle built high above behind ramparts, and was where the stablemen lived.*

All statues, inside and out, were to be destroyed. Eight statues of apostles in the nave and seven in the North Porch were in fact taken down, and it was even suggested that the entire cathedral should be demolished. Certain citizens, however, disapproved, including the architect Morin, who pointed out the difficulties involved!

By 1795 the danger had passed, and in 1800, on the feast day of the Assumption, Mass was once more celebrated in the cathedral of Our Lady of Chartres.

The 19th and 20th centuries

The vast wooden framework, known as 'la forêt', above the stone vaults, which had been stripped of its lead tiling during the Revolution, was now re-covered, but on 4 June 1836, due to the carelessness of workmen, a great fire destroyed all the wooden roof structures over the nave, choir and transept. Fortunately, the stone vaults withstood the calamity, and a new cast-iron framework, covered with copper, was completed by 1841.

During the 1870–71 war Chartres was occupied by the Prussians. Although only slightly bombed during the 1914–18 war, it suffered more in the Second World War, especially on 26 May 1944, when the Town Hall was hit, and a priceless library of medieval manuscripts was lost. During both world wars, however, the cathedral glass was removed, and has survived intact. Jean Moulin, Prefect of Eure-et-Loir, distinguished himself as the principal organiser of the French Resistance, and died as a result of Nazi torture. Before retreating, Hitler's troops blew up William's Gate, and burnt St Andrew's Church.

Since 1963 a vast programme of restoration and preservation has been undertaken, both at the cathedral and in the town. The most deteriorated statues of the Royal Portal have been taken down and placed in the crypt, and copies installed in their places. The three great 12th-century lancets of the west façade were totally cleaned, restored and releaded between 1974 and 1976 and work has now begun on

the restoration of the 13th-century glass.

At the same time, painstakingly, with the help of State and municipal grants, street by street, house by house, the Old Town of Chartres is being renovated, from St Peter's to St Andrew's, along the river, and up to the cathedral, by the rue Saint-Pierre, rue du Bourg, rue des Ecuyers and the rue Chantault.

Thus, even today, as throughout the centuries, in war and in peace, in times of adversity and of prosperity alike, the history and destiny of Chartres, its people and its cathedral, are still interwoven.

★

ABOVE: *A mother and her child lighting a candle to the Virgin in the cathedral.*

★

All photographs in this book are © Sonia Halliday and Laura Lushington and were taken with Pentax 6 × 7 equipment.

SBN 85372 333 8